Animal Top Tens

South America's Most Amazing Animals

Anita Ganeri

www.raintreepublishers.co.uk
Visit our website to find out more information about Raintree books.

To order:
☎ Phone 44 (0) 1865 888112
▤ Send a fax to 44 (0) 1865 314091
▢ Visit the Raintree Bookshop at www.raintreepublishers.co.uk to browse our catalogue and order online

First published in Great Britain by Raintree,
Halley Court, Jordan Hill, Oxford OX2 8EJ, part of Harcourt Education.
Raintree is a registered trademark of Harcourt Education Ltd.

Editorial: Nancy Dickmann and Catherine Veitch
Design: Victoria Bevan and Geoff Ward
Illustrations: Geoff Ward
Picture Research: Mica Brancic
Production: Victoria Fitzgerald

Originated by Modern Age
Printed and bound by CTPS (China Translation & Printing Services Ltd)

13-digit ISBN 978 1 4062 0922 8
12 11 10 09 08
10 9 8 7 6 5 4 3 2 1

British Library Cataloguing in Publication Data
Ganeri, Anita, 1961-
    South America's Most Amazing Animals.
(Animal top tens)
591.9'8
A full catalogue record for this book is available from the British Library.

Acknowledgements
The author and publisher are grateful to the following for permission to reproduce copyright material: ©Ardea pp. 6, 17 (Francois Gohier), 18, 19, 20 (M. Watson); ©FLPA pp. 4 (Fritz Polking), 27 (Krystyna Szulecka); ©FLPA/Foto Natura/SA Team p. 7; ©FLPA/Minden Pictures pp. 10, 11, 13 (Michael & Patricia Fogden), 12 (Mark Moffett), 14 (Christian Ziegler), 16 (Claus Meyer), 21, 25 (Tui De Roy), 26 (Pete Oxford); ©OSF pp. 8 (Roy Toft), 9, 22 (Juniors Bildarchiv); ©OSF/Oxford Scientific p. 15; ©OSF/Tartan Dragon p. 24 (Doug Allan).

Cover photograph of a poison-arrow frog, reproduced with permission of Naturepl.com/Mark Payne-Gill.

The publishers would like to thank Michael Bright for his assistance with the preparation of this book.

Every effort has been made to contact copyright holders of any material reproduced in this book. Any omissions will be rectified in subsequent printings if notice is given to the publishers.

Contents

Some words are printed in bold, **like this**. You can find out what they mean on page 31 in the Glossary.

South America

South America is the world's fourth largest **continent,** covering about 18,000,000 sq kilometres (6,948,000 sq miles). The Pacific Ocean lies to the west. The Atlantic Ocean lies to the east. There are several groups of islands off the coast. They include Tierra del Fuego and the Galapagos Islands.

South America has many different kinds of landscape. **Tropical rainforests** cover over a third of the continent. The largest is the Amazon rainforest. It grows along the Amazon River, the world's second longest river. There are also vast plains called **grasslands,** great lakes and waterfalls, baking deserts, and high mountain ranges.

There are 275 waterfalls along the Iguacu River. Some are as high as 82 metres (269 feet).

Key
- rainforest
- mountains
- swamp
- grassland
- desert

0   500 miles
0   500 kilometres

An amazing range of animals lives in these **habitats**. The rainforests are home to thousands of creatures, including jaguars, howler monkeys, and sloths. Magnificent birds of prey fly high above the Andes mountains. Fish, such as piranhas, swim in the rivers. These animals have special features to help them survive in their particular homes.

Jaguar

The jaguar is the biggest cat and **mammal** in South America. It lives in the **rainforests**. Jaguars sleep during the day. They hunt at dawn and dusk when most of the animals they eat are also on the move.

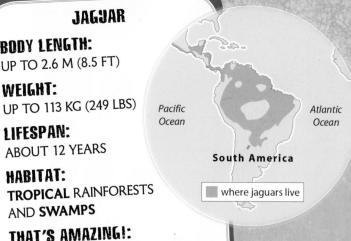

JAGUAR

BODY LENGTH:
UP TO 2.6 M (8.5 FT)

WEIGHT:
UP TO 113 KG (249 LBS)

LIFESPAN:
ABOUT 12 YEARS

HABITAT:
TROPICAL RAINFORESTS AND **SWAMPS**

THAT'S AMAZING!:
JAGUARS DO NOT ROAR LIKE LIONS AND TIGERS. THEY GRUNT WHEN THEY ARE HUNTING, AND THEY CAN ALSO GROWL.

Pacific Ocean

Atlantic Ocean

South America

□ where jaguars live

A jaguar's powerful legs are good for climbing forest trees.

Along with tigers, jaguars are the only big cats that enjoy swimming.

Camouflage

The jaguar has a stunning golden coat, covered with black spots. These markings help to hide the jaguar in the forest.

Built for hunting

The jaguar has a strong body, powerful paws and sharp teeth for hunting. It catches forest animals, such as wild pigs, deer, monkeys, birds, and fish. It kills its **prey** with a bite to the throat. Jaguars are good at climbing trees but usually stalk their prey on the ground. Sometimes they crouch by the riverbank and wait for fish to swim past.

Howler monkey

Howler monkeys live high up in the trees of the **rainforest**. They get their name from the loud sounds they make. The sound is so loud that it can be heard up to 5 kilometres (3.1 miles) away. This makes the howler monkey the loudest animal and **mammal** on land.

Howler monkeys feed on leaves, fruit and flowers in the treetops.

HOWLER MONKEY

BODY LENGTH:
50–65 CM (20–25 IN)

TAIL LENGTH:
50–70 CM (20–27 IN)

WEIGHT:
UP TO 7 KG (15.4 LBS)

LIFESPAN:
15–20 YEARS

HABITAT:
TROPICAL RAINFORESTS

THAT'S AMAZING!:
HOWLER MONKEYS HAVE LONG,
STRONG TAILS WHICH THEY USE
TO GRIP ON TO TREE BRANCHES
AS THEY ARE FEEDING.

Pacific Ocean

Atlantic Ocean

South America

☐ where howler monkeys live

The monkeys' "howl" is more like a roaring sound.

Defending space

Howler monkeys live in **troops** of about
10-15 monkeys. Each troop has its own space
where it lives and feeds. Every morning and
evening, the monkeys begin to howl. Their call is returned
by other troops living nearby. By doing this, the troops can
find out where each other is and keep out of each other's way.
Making loud sounds is a good way to communicate in the
rainforest where it can be hard to see other animals.

Sloth

Sloths spend most of their lives hanging upside down. They hang high up in the branches of the trees in the **rainforest,** in an area known as the **canopy.** A sloth moves very slowly and may stay in the same tree for years, feeding on leaves. A sloth only climbs down to the ground once a week to go to the toilet.

Some sloths have two claws on each hand. Other sloths have three claws.

Life in the trees

Sloths are well **adapted** for life in the rainforest. Unlike the hair of any other **mammal**, a sloth's fur grows from its stomach down towards its back. This allows rain to run off more easily. Long, hook-like claws help the sloth to cling to the branches. It also uses its claws to defend itself from enemies, such as jaguars and eagles.

SLOTH

BODY LENGTH:
UP TO 60 CM (23.4 IN)

WEIGHT:
UP TO 4 KG
(8.75 LBS)

LIFESPAN:
UP TO 12 YEARS

HABITAT:
TROPICAL RAINFORESTS

THAT'S AMAZING!:
SLOTHS SLEEP FOR 15–18 HOURS A DAY, HANGING UPSIDE DOWN FROM A BRANCH.

Pacific Ocean

Atlantic Ocean

South America

☐ where sloths live

A sloth's brown fur often looks green because tiny plants live in it.

Poison-arrow frog

Poison-arrow frogs are tiny, brightly coloured frogs that live in the **rainforest**. They spend most of their time on the forest floor. They hunt for ants, termites, and other small **insects** that live among the fallen leaves.

There are many different kinds and colours of poison-arrow frogs.

Warning colours
In nature, bright colours, such as red, yellow, black, and green, are a warning sign. A frog's bright colours warn other animals that it is poisonous to eat. Some frogs have such strong poison that one drop could kill a monkey.

POISON-ARROW FROG

BODY LENGTH:
1–6 CM (0.39–2.36 IN)

LIFESPAN:
5–12 YEARS
(IN **CAPTIVITY**)

HABITAT:
TROPICAL RAINFORESTS

THAT'S AMAZING!:
LOCAL PEOPLE USED TO PUT FROG POISON ON THE TIPS OF THEIR HUNTING ARROWS. THAT'S HOW THE FROGS GOT THEIR NAME.

South America

Pacific Ocean

Atlantic Ocean

where poison-arrow frogs live

Rainwater collects on leaves. The frogs eat insects that fall into the water.

Plant pools

Some kinds of poison-arrow frogs are good parents. The female lays her eggs on a leaf. When the eggs hatch, the tadpoles usually climb onto the male's back. He carries them to a pool of rainwater inside a **bromeliad** plant. This keeps them safe from hungry enemies. The tadpoles eat insects that fall into the water. After about a month, they turn into frogs.

Army ants

Army ants are tiny, golden-brown **insects**. They mostly live on the **rainforest** floor. They live in enormous "armies". By working together, the ants can catch and kill **prey** which is much bigger than themselves.

ARMY ANT

BODY LENGTH:
3–12 MM
(0.11–0.46 IN)

LIFESPAN:
SEVERAL MONTHS
(WORKER ANTS);
SEVERAL YEARS
(QUEENS)

HABITAT:
TROPICAL RAINFORESTS

THAT'S AMAZING!:
ARMY ANTS SOMETIMES RAID PEOPLE'S HOMES, BUT THIS CAN BE USEFUL BECAUSE THE ANTS EAT UP INSECT PESTS.

Pacific Ocean

Atlantic Ocean

South America

where army ants live

There can be at least 2 million ants in an army.

When they are not marching, the ants live in nests mostly on the ground.

Ants on the move

Army ants march long distances through the forest to find food, such as wasps, cockroaches, and crickets. They sting their prey to death and pull it apart with their jaws. Then they can carry it back to their nest. When ants find food, they give out a strong smell. The other ants recognise the smell and know to gather round and attack.

Army ants cannot see very well. Some of the ants wipe their bodies on the ground to mark it with a strong smell. Other ants recognise the smell and know which trail to follow.

Anaconda

The anaconda lives in slow-moving rivers and **swamps**. It is the world's biggest snake.

The anaconda's dull green and black colouring helps to hide it among the plants and the dark water.

ANACONDA

BODY LENGTH:
UP TO 9 M (29.5 FT)

WEIGHT:
UP TO 200 KG
(440 LBS)

LIFESPAN:
10–30 YEARS

HABITAT:
RIVERS AND SWAMPS

THAT'S AMAZING!:
IT TAKES AN ANACONDA SEVERAL WEEKS TO DIGEST A BIG MEAL. AFTER A BIG MEAL IT MAY NOT NEED TO EAT AGAIN FOR SEVERAL MONTHS.

Pacific Ocean

Atlantic Ocean

South America

☐ where anacondas live

Life in the water

The anaconda spends most of its time in the water. It lies and waits for animals, such as deer, wild boar, and goats, to come to the water to drink. Then the snake grabs the animal in its jaws. The snake pulls it underwater and coils around it, crushing it to death.

An anaconda's eyes and nostrils are on top of its head. This allows it to see and breathe as it lies in the water. Anacondas are fast swimmers and they can also climb trees to escape from enemies.

Anaconda swallow their **prey** whole.

Piranha

Piranhas are small fish which live in slow-moving rivers and streams. They might be small but some kinds are famous for being fierce feeders. They find their **prey** by smell or movement, then they quickly swim towards it. Piranhas mostly eat other fish, stripping their bodies to the bone. They also feed on the bodies of dead animals.

PIRANHA

BODY LENGTH:
UP TO 40 CM (15.7 IN)

WEIGHT:
UP TO 3.5 KG (7.7 LBS)

HABITAT:
SLOW-MOVING RIVERS AND STREAMS

THAT'S AMAZING!:
SOME KINDS OF PIRANHAS ARE VEGETARIANS! THEY USE THEIR SHARP TEETH TO CRACK NUTS WHICH FALL IN THE WATER.

Atlantic Ocean

Orinoco River

Amazon River

Pacific Ocean

South America

São Francisco River

Paraná River

where piranhas live

At dawn and dusk, large **shoals** of piranhas gather to wait for prey.

A piranha's teeth are triangular and sit close together in its mouth.

Terrifying teeth

A piranha's jaws are lined with blade-like teeth, sharp enough to bite through a metal fishing hook. They are used for biting and tearing, and can easily take large chunks of flesh out of a bigger fish. The piranha's lower jaw sticks out further than its upper jaw. This makes its teeth fit together like a trap.

Andean condor

The Andean condor is one of the largest flying birds in the world. It lives in the Andes mountain range. It uses its huge wings to **soar** high on air which rises over the mountains.

The Andean condor feeds on dead animals such as deer and cattle. It searches for its food as it soars in the sky.

ANDEAN CONDOR

BODY HEIGHT:
1.3 M (4.2 FT)

WINGSPAN:
UP TO 3 M (9.8 FT)

WEIGHT:
9–12 KG (19.8–26.4 LBS)

LIFESPAN:
ABOUT 50 YEARS

HABITAT:
GRASSLAND AND MOUNTAINS

THAT'S AMAZING!:
YOUNG CONDORS CAN FLY WHEN THEY ARE SIX MONTHS OLD, BUT THEY STAY AND HUNT WITH THEIR PARENTS UNTIL THEY ARE ABOUT ONE AND A HALF YEARS OLD.

Atlantic Ocean

South America

Pacific Ocean

☐ where Andean condors live

A condor uses its outstanding eyesight to spot food from a great height.

The male Andean condor is different from the female. It has a large comb and wattle.

comb

wattle

Unusual appearance

Andean condors are mostly black with white patches on their wings and a white ruff around their necks. But they have bare skin on their faces and necks. This allows them to poke their head and beak into the animals they are eating without getting their feathers dirty.

Giant anteater

The giant anteater is an odd-looking **mammal**. It has a long, pointed head, long, sharp claws, and a long, bushy tail. But each of its body features is designed for its way of life.

GIANT ANTEATER

BODY LENGTH:
1–1.3 M (3.28–4.2 FT)

TAIL LENGTH:
65–90 CM
(25.3–35.1 IN)

WEIGHT:
22–40 KG (48.4–88 LBS)

LIFESPAN:
UP TO 26 YEARS
(IN CAPTIVITY)

HABITAT:
GRASSLANDS, WOODLANDS, TROPICAL RAINFORESTS, SWAMPS

THAT'S AMAZING!:
AN ANTEATER CAN FLICK ITS TONGUE IN AND OUT AS MANY AS 150 TIMES A MINUTE.

Pacific Ocean

South America

Atlantic Ocean

☐ where giant anteaters live

An anteater's claws are so long that it has to walk on the sides of its feet.

Body design

The giant anteater feeds on the ants and termites that make their nests in its **habitat.** It must eat more than 20,000 ants a day to survive. The giant anteater uses its long claws to break an ants' nest open. Then it flicks its long, sticky tongue in and out to lick up the ants.

A giant anteater rests for up to 15 hours a day in a hollow in the ground. As it sleeps, it covers its body with its bushy tail.

Marine iguana

Marine iguanas live on the rocky coasts around the Galapagos Islands. They are the only lizards that feed in the sea. They have flattened tails for swimming and strong claws for gripping on to the slippery rocks.

MARINE IGUANA

BODY AND TAIL LENGTH:
UP TO 1.5 M (4.9 FT)

WEIGHT:
UP TO 1.5 KG (3.3 LBS)

LIFESPAN:
5–12 YEARS

HABITAT:
ROCKY COASTS

THAT'S AMAZING!:
MARINE IGUANAS OFTEN SNEEZE TO GET RID OF SALT FROM THEIR NOSES. THEY TAKE IN SALTY SEA WATER AS THEY FEED, AND TOO MUCH SALT IN THEIR BODIES CAN KILL THEM.

□ where marine iguanas live

Atlantic Ocean

Pacific Ocean

Galapagos Islands

South America

Marine iguanas live in large groups for most of the year.

Seaweed grazers

Marine iguanas eat seaweed that grows on rocks in the water. They dive into the sea to feed. They have small, razor-sharp teeth for scraping seaweed off the rocks. They chew with one side of their mouths, then with the other, like a dog chewing on a bone.

When feeding, marine iguanas can stay underwater for up to an hour and a half.

Cold-blooded

Like most **reptiles**, marine iguanas are **cold-blooded**. They have to warm their bodies up in the sun to be active. They sunbathe in the morning and in between dips into the cold sea.

Animals in danger

Many kinds of animals in South America are in danger of dying out forever. When an animal dies out, it is said to be **extinct.** Many animals are dying out because people are destroying their **habitats.** Other animals are hunted for their meat or skins.

The hyacinth macaw lives in the Amazon **rainforest** and Pantanal **swamps.** It lives and feeds from just a few kinds of trees. Many of these trees are being cut down. If this continues the hyacinth macaw will become extinct. Thousands of these birds have also been caught for their beautiful blue feathers and for sale as pets.

The beautiful hyacinth macaw is the world's largest parrot, growing a metre (3.3 feet) tall.

A giant tortoise can live for more than 150 years.

The giant tortoise of the Galapagos Islands can weigh more than 200 kg (440 lbs). In the past, so many tortoises were killed for their meat that they almost died out. Today they face a new threat. Now the tortoises have to compete for food with animals such as goats and cattle, which people brought to the islands.

Today, **conservation** groups are working hard to save these amazing animals.

Animal facts and figures

There are millions of different kinds of animals living all over the world. The place where an animal lives is called its **habitat**. Animals have special features, such as wings, claws, and fins. These features allow animals to survive in their habitats. Which animal do you think is the most amazing?

JAGUAR

BODY LENGTH:
UP TO 2.6 M (8.5 FT)

WEIGHT:
UP TO 113 KG (249 LBS)

LIFESPAN:
ABOUT 12 YEARS

HABITAT:
TROPICAL RAINFORESTS AND SWAMPS

THAT'S AMAZING!:
JAGUARS DO NOT ROAR LIKE LIONS AND TIGERS. THEY GRUNT WHEN THEY ARE HUNTING, AND THEY CAN ALSO GROWL.

HOWLER MONKEY

BODY LENGTH:
50–65 CM (20–25 IN)

TAIL LENGTH:
50–70 CM (20–27 IN)

WEIGHT:
UP TO 7 KG (15.4 LBS)

LIFESPAN:
15–20 YEARS

HABITAT:
TROPICAL RAINFORESTS

THAT'S AMAZING!:
HOWLER MONKEYS HAVE LONG, STRONG TAILS WHICH THEY USE TO GRIP ON TO TREE BRANCHES AS THEY ARE FEEDING.

SLOTH

BODY LENGTH:
UP TO 60 CM (23.4 IN)

WEIGHT:
UP TO 4 KG (8.75 LBS)

LIFESPAN:
UP TO 12 YEARS

HABITAT:
TROPICAL RAINFORESTS

THAT'S AMAZING!:
SLOTHS SLEEP FOR 15–18 HOURS A DAY, HANGING UPSIDE DOWN FROM A BRANCH.

POISON-ARROW FROG

BODY LENGTH:
1–6 CM (0.39–2.36 IN)

LIFESPAN:
5–12 YEARS (IN **CAPTIVITY**)

HABITAT:
TROPICAL RAINFORESTS

THAT'S AMAZING!:
LOCAL PEOPLE USED TO PUT FROG POISON ON THE TIPS OF THEIR HUNTING ARROWS. THAT'S HOW THE FROGS GOT THEIR NAME.

ARMY ANT

BODY LENGTH:
3–12 MM (0.11–0.46 IN)

LIFESPAN:
SEVERAL MONTHS (WORKER ANTS); SEVERAL YEARS (QUEENS)

HABITAT:
TROPICAL RAINFORESTS

THAT'S AMAZING!:
ARMY ANTS SOMETIMES RAID PEOPLE'S HOMES, BUT THIS CAN BE USEFUL BECAUSE THE ANTS EAT UP **INSECT** PESTS.

ANACONDA

BODY LENGTH:
UP TO 9 M (29.5 FT)

WEIGHT:
UP TO 200 KG (440 LBS)

LIFESPAN:
10–30 YEARS

HABITAT:
RIVERS AND SWAMPS

THAT'S AMAZING!:
IT TAKES AN ANACONDA SEVERAL WEEKS TO DIGEST A BIG MEAL. AFTER A BIG MEAL IT MAY NOT NEED TO EAT AGAIN FOR SEVERAL MONTHS.

PIRANHA

BODY LENGTH:
UP TO 40 CM (15.7 IN)

WEIGHT:
UP TO 3.5 KG (7.7 LBS)

HABITAT:
SLOW-MOVING RIVERS AND STREAMS

THAT'S AMAZING!:
SOME KINDS OF PIRANHAS ARE VEGETARIANS! THEY USE THEIR SHARP TEETH TO CRACK NUTS WHICH FALL IN THE WATER.

ANDEAN CONDOR

BODY HEIGHT:
1.3 M (4.2 FT)

WINGSPAN:
UP TO 3 M (9.8 FT)

WEIGHT:
9–12 KG (19.8–26.4 LBS)

LIFESPAN:
ABOUT 50 YEARS

HABITAT:
GRASSLAND AND MOUNTAINS

THAT'S AMAZING!:
YOUNG CONDORS CAN FLY WHEN THEY ARE SIX MONTHS OLD, BUT THEY STAY AND HUNT WITH THEIR PARENTS UNTIL THEY ARE ABOUT ONE AND A HALF YEARS OLD.

GIANT ANTEATER

BODY LENGTH:
1–1.3 M (3.28–4.2 FT)

TAIL LENGTH:
65–90 CM (25.3–35.1 IN)

WEIGHT:
22–40 KG (48.4–88 LBS)

LIFESPAN:
UP TO 26 YEARS (IN **CAPTIVITY**)

HABITAT:
GRASSLANDS, WOODLANDS, TROPICAL RAINFORESTS, SWAMPS

THAT'S AMAZING!:
AN ANTEATER CAN FLICK ITS TONGUE IN AND OUT AS MANY AS 150 TIMES A MINUTE.

MARINE IGUANA

BODY AND TAIL LENGTH:
UP TO 1.5 M (4.9 FT)

WEIGHT:
UP TO 1.5 KG (3.3 LBS)

LIFESPAN:
5–12 YEARS

HABITAT:
ROCKY COASTS

THAT'S AMAZING!:
MARINE IGUANAS OFTEN SNEEZE TO GET RID OF SALT FROM THEIR NOSES. THEY TAKE IN SALTY SEA WATER AS THEY FEED, AND TOO MUCH SALT IN THEIR BODIES CAN KILL THEM.

Find out more

Books to read

Exploring Continents: South America, Anita Ganeri (Heinemann Library, 2007)

Living Things: Adaptation, Holly Wallace (Heinemann Library, 2001)

Living Things: Survival and Change, Holly Wallace (Heinemann Library, 2001)

Websites

http://www.bbc.co.uk/nature/reallywild
Type in the name of the animal you want to learn about and find a page with lots of facts, figures, and pictures.

http://animals.nationalgeographic.com/animals
This site has information on the different groups of animals, stories of survival in different habitats, and stunning photo galleries to search through.

http://animaldiversity.ummz.umich.edu
A website run by the University of Michigan which has a huge encyclopedia of animals to search through.

http://www.mnh.si.edu
The website of the Smithsonian National Museum of Natural History, which has one of the largest natural history collections in the world.

Zoo sites
Many zoos around the world have their own websites which tell you about the animals they keep, where they come from, and how they are looked after.

Glossary

adapted when an animal has special features that help it to survive in its habitat

bromeliad rainforest plant that grows above the ground on a branch of a tree

canopy thick layer of treetops where most rainforest animals live

captivity animals kept in a zoo or wildlife park live in captivity. Animals in captivity often live longer than wild animals because they have no predators, nor competition for food.

cold-blooded animal that cannot control its body temperature but relies on the weather to cool it down or warm it up

conservation saving and protecting threatened animals and habitats

continent one of seven huge pieces of land on Earth. Each continent is divided into smaller regions called countries.

extinct when a kind of animal dies out forever

grassland huge, open space covered in grass and bushes

habitat place where an animal lives and feeds

insect animal with six legs and three parts to its body

mammal animal that has fur or hair and feeds its babies on milk

prey animals that are hunted and killed by other animals for food

rainforest thick forest growing around the Equator where the weather is hot and wet

reptile animal with scaly skin that lays eggs on land

shoal large group of fish

soar when a bird flies through the air without flapping its wings

swamp area where large parts of the land are usually waterlogged

troop group of monkeys

tropical places around the equator which are hot and wet all year round

Index